Silver Matilda

The 'Get to Know Me' series is aimed at children with additional needs and those who support them in the classroom. Developed by child psychologist Dr Louise Lightfoot and illustrated by Catherine Hicks, the resources in this series include activities specific to anxiety, depression and Obsessive Compulsive Disorder (OCD). This book, *Silver Matilda*, has been designed to support the individual child but also to be used in whole class teaching, to encourage an empathetic and inclusive environment.

In this book, we meet Silver Matilda, a bird with silver feathers known for her beauty and graceful flight. The story follows Matilda as she loses her bright feathers and, ashamed, hides away from the world until one day an owl comes and sits with her. The owl shows Matilda empathy and stays with her whilst she recovers and watches as she becomes stronger through her experience.

This book was written with children with depression in mind, providing an opportunity to relate to Matilda's thoughts, feelings, behaviours and experiences. However, children with a range of needs may benefit from the story. The book is written in a narrative style, so it does not use diagnostic labels and is not intended for this purpose. Instead the focus is on creating a common language which children can understand and use to make sense of how they are feeling.

A practitioner guidebook (ISBN 978-0-8153-4943-3) and draw along version (ISBN 978-0-8153-4946-4) are also available.

Dr Louise Lightfoot is an Educational and Child Psychologist working with children and young people aged 0–25. She holds a BA in Educational Studies, MEd in the Psychology of Education and doctorate in Educational and Child Psychology. Louise has worked in a variety of settings ranging from mainstream schools to secure units and psychiatric facilities, and has a special interest in working to empower at risk or 'hard to reach' groups. As a person who suffers with Ehlers Danlos, stroke and dyslexia, she has a first-hand understanding of the frustrations and difficulties that accompany a specific physical or learning difficulty. Louise currently works as an HCPC registered Independent Psychologist. If you would like to discuss working with her, please contact Louise at: louise.lightfoot@hotmail.co.uk.

Catherine Hicks is an East Yorkshire artist, illustrator, wife and mother. She spent 13 years as a Registered Veterinary Nurse before injury and chronic illnesses led to her creative hobby becoming therapy. When Catherine and Louise were introduced, it was obvious they were kindred spirits and from there the Get to Know Me Series was born.

T0002678

GET TO KNOW ME SERIES

Series author: Dr Louise Lightfoot
Illustrated by: Catherine Hicks

The **'Get to Know Me'** series is a series of resources aimed at children with SEN or EBD and the professionals who support them in the mainstream primary classroom. Each resource concentrates on a different condition and comprises of three titles, available separately.

A **traditional children's picture book** – designed to support the individual child but also to be used in whole class teaching, to encourage an empathetic and inclusive environment.

An **interactive workbook**. This is a workbook version of the story in which individual children are encouraged to interact with the story in a creative way – through writing, drawing, scrap booking, collage, activities etc. (templates and cut outs will be made available online). Children are more likely to understand and process information if they have had to actively engage with it. The workbook will aid long-term recall and increase the level of understanding.

A **practitioner guide** created for key adults (teachers, therapists and parents) by a child psychologist, with activities specific to each condition. These activities will link to the books and offer practical tools and strategies to support the child and those around them in addition to the information specific to the condition to improve understanding of a child's needs to promote empathy and acceptance.

https://www.routledge.com/Get-To-Know-Me/book-series/GKM

Books included in this series:

Set 1 Get to Know Me: Anxiety
Available as a set and individual books

Book 1
Supporting Children with Anxiety to Understand and Celebrate Difference
A Get to Know Me Workbook and Guide for Parents and Practitioners
PB 978-0-8153-4941-9
eBook 978-1-351-16492-4

Book 2
Sammy Sloth
Get to Know Me: Anxiety
PB 978-0-8153-4953-2
eBook 978-1-351-16452-8

Book 3
Draw Along With Sammy Sloth
Get to Know Me: Anxiety
PB 978-0-8153-4942-6
eBook 978-1-351-16484-9

Set 2 Get to Know Me: Depression
Available as a set and individual books

Book 1
Supporting Children with Depression to Understand and Celebrate Difference
A Get to Know Me Workbook and Guide for Parents and Practitioners
PB 978-0-8153-4943-3
eBook 978-1-351-16480-1

Book 2
Silver Matilda
Get to Know Me: Depression
PB 978-0-8153-4945-7
eBook 978-1-351-16476-4

Book 3
Draw Along With Silver Matilda
Get to Know Me: Depression
PB 978-0-8153-4946-4
eBook 978-1-351-16472-6

Set 3 Get to Know Me: OCD
Available as a set and individual books

Book 1
Supporting Children with OCD to Understand and Celebrate Difference
A Get to Know Me Workbook and Guide for Parents and Practitioners
PB 978-0-8153-4948-8
eBook 978-1-351-16468-9

Book 2
Tidy Tim
Get to Know Me: OCD
PB 978-0-8153-4950-1
eBook 978-1-351-16460-3

Book 3
Draw Along With Tidy Tim
Get to Know Me: OCD
PB 978-0-8153-4951-8
eBook 978-1-351-16456-6

SILVER MATILDA

GET TO KNOW ME: DEPRESSION

DR LOUISE LIGHTFOOT

ILLUSTRATED BY CATHERINE HICKS

Routledge
Taylor & Francis Group

LONDON AND NEW YORK

First published 2020
by Routledge
2 Park Square, Milton Park, Abingdon, Oxon OX14 4RN

and by Routledge
52 Vanderbilt Avenue, New York, NY 10017

Routledge is an imprint of the Taylor & Francis Group, an informa business

British Library Cataloguing-in-Publication Data
A catalogue record for this book is available from the British Library

Library of Congress Cataloging-in-Publication Data
A catalog record has been requested for this book

ISBN: 978-0-8153-4945-7 (pbk)
ISBN: 978-1-351-16476-4 (ebk)

Typeset in Stone Informal
by Apex CoVantage, LLC

DEDICATIONS

From Louise:

For Natasha,

Who flew too quickly but who shone ever so bright. I'll do my best in the name of Lasha and in the hope of giving others flight.

And for Matilda,

Do you Tildatron! You are ace! to your parents - Ben, thank you for collaboration, you started this ball rolling with me and I hope one day we get work together again, you are one talented and kind-hearted guy! And Rach, not only does your involvement legitimatise my life! But your supervision and faith in my abilities helped my feathers stay on as long as they did and grow back as quickly as they did.

From Catherine:

To Dianne and Peter Davies, a.k.a. Mum and Dad, who have always been there for me to love and guide me – you are amazing!

I must give a special shout out to my mum, from whom I inherited my creative and artistic ability and because she has tirelessly encouraged, supported and inspired me throughout this process.

CONTENTS

Acknowledgements

To Katrina my editor, thank you for taking a chance and sticking with us, especially during our particularly 'imperfectly flawed' moments! You have been a wonderful source of personal support and a professional wisdom.

Professor Kevin Woods for your (I often wondered if misguided) belief in me and continued support. Here's to being a square peg in a round hole.

The University of Manchester and the students of the Doctorate of Educational Psychology Course, in particular Jill and Ben Simpson, for their collaboration, perspective and belief.

Huge thank you for the contributions to: Dr Lindsay 'grammar' Kay, Dr Katie Pierce, Dr Richard Skelton, Dr Rachael Hornsby, Dr Rachel Lyons and Jade Charelson for their professional insight, unwavering friendship, invaluable contribution and time. You really are the Waitrose of Psychologists (quality wise, not overpriced!).

Thank you to all my family and friends who have endured numerous versions of these books and for their support during the periods in which I was very ill and gained tenacity from believing I could make something good come out of it all.

To Erin and Drew for being excellent guinea pigs and the source of great inspiration. To Owen for being a friend to me at 13 and 35 with admittedly slightly improved cooking skills. To Dianne Davies for her experience, support and knowledge of the area which helped more than you could know.

Thanks to Catherine Hicks, my illustrator, the gin to my tonic! Perhaps in finding each other we made two slightly broken people whole.

To all my Zebra friends and those who have overcome adversity, keep going. Big up to Ellie Taylor for representing the herd!

A huge thank you to Tim Watson for your supervision, guidance and support. You have helped me realise my potential when I couldn't see it in myself. You are an excellent critical friend, fountain of knowledge and all round lovely person!

Thanks for my Dad for always believing in me and constantly filling my freezer and thanks to my big brother John, who annoyed me as a child and who has always been there for me as an adult.

To the Hickling family, I couldn't have wished to marry into a better family, your support love and acceptance of me as a Scouser is forever appreciated.

Thank you to Jonathan Merrett, the copy editor, for his patience and flexibility and to Leah Burton, my Editorial Assistant, for her help along the way.

Finally, a huge thank you to Gillian Steadman, my Senior Production Editor, who is the yin to my yang. Couldn't have done this without you!

Silver Matilda – A picture book story

There once was bird
She was awesome and bright,
You might think her a star
If you saw her at night.

Her name was Matilda,
And everyone knew
Of this beautiful bird
And all she could do.

Her eyes were like diamonds
That glistened and shone,
With a waterfall tail
That flowed on and on.

She danced on the clouds
And breezed through the sky;
She swirled and she twirled
And she fluttered on by.

You could not forget her
Once you'd seen her go by;
You could only be dazzled
As she'd brighten the sky.

She bathed in the sunlight
On a bright summer's day,
Preening her feathers
Shining silvery grey.

She noticed a feather
Fall down to the floor;
She scrambled in panic
Afraid to see more.

And tears filled her eyes
As she looked all around
At the glistening trail
That littered the ground.

And that's how it started;
On that very day
Matilda could feel herself
Fading away.

She didn't feel bright
Now she felt very small;
Now she didn't feel a bit like
Matilda at all.

So she sat in a huddle
Trying to hide in her wings;
Away from the world
And all troubling things.

But now all her feathers
Had fallen away,
She was no longer silver
She only felt grey.

So she sat all alone
For the longest of whiles,
And felt far away
From a world full of smiles.

Then, all of a sudden,
She heard a voice say,
"Hello there Matilda
Are you hiding away?"

She felt so embarrassed;
"Please close your eyes,
I'm Silver Matilda,
the Queen of the skies.

"You can't see me like this
I'm broken and small.
I've lost all my feathers
Now I'm nothing at all."

"I'm Owen," said the owl
Who sat down by her side.
"Well, I see a bird
Who is hurting inside.

"Don't feel afraid,
As from time to time
We all feel alone
And we might lose our shine.

"So we might need a friend
To help us find light,
Or simply to be there
As long as it's night."

And as the time passed
The owl didn't go,
He sat by her side
Until there was snow.

And the world filled with colour
And was no longer grey,
She felt herself change
And night turned to day.

Her heart filled with love
Knowing someone did care,
Though she didn't look up
She knew Owen was there.

And that's when she noticed
Feathers starting to sprout,
All this time she'd been hiding
It was time to come out.

So she pulled back her wings
And saw friendly eyes,
And then her reflection
Oh what a surprise!

She couldn't believe it,
It gave her a fright.
She looked like Matilda
But now she was bright.

And the owl had helped
Re-light the spark,
And saw her shine
When she felt only dark.

And her heart was changed forever
By the kindness of another
Who brought her back from sadness
And helped her to recover.

She glimmered and shimmered,
Such a figure to behold,
She was no longer silver,
Now Matilda, she was gold.

SILVER MATILDA – TEXT ONLY VERSION

There once was bird
She was awesome and bright,
You might think her a star
If you saw her at night.

Her name was Matilda,
And everyone knew
Of this beautiful bird
And all she could do.

Her eyes were like diamonds
That glistened and shone,
With a waterfall tail
That flowed on and on.

She danced on the clouds
And breezed through the sky;
She swirled and she twirled
And she fluttered on by.

You could not forget her
Once you'd seen her go by;
You could only be dazzled
As she'd brighten the sky.

She bathed in the sunlight
On a bright summer's day,
Preening her feathers
Shining silvery grey.

She noticed a feather
Fall down to the floor;
She scrambled in panic
Afraid to see more.

And tears filled her eyes
As she looked all around
At the glistening trail
That littered the ground.

And that's how it started;
On that very day
Matilda could feel herself
Fading away.

She didn't feel bright
Now she felt very small;
Now she didn't feel a bit like
Matilda at all.

So she sat in a huddle
Trying to hide in her wings;
Away from the world
And all troubling things.

But now all her feathers
Had fallen away,
She was no longer silver
She only felt grey.

So she sat all alone
For the longest of whiles,
And felt far away
From a world full of smiles.

Then, all of a sudden,
She heard a voice say,
"Hello there Matilda
Are you hiding away?"

She felt so embarrassed;
"Please close your eyes,
I'm Silver Matilda,
the Queen of the skies.

"You can't see me like this
I'm broken and small.
I've lost all my feathers
Now I'm nothing at all."

"I'm Owen," said the owl
Who sat down by her side.
"Well, I see a bird
Who is hurting inside.

"Don't feel afraid,
As from time to time
We all feel alone
And we might lose our shine.

"So we might need a friend
To help us find light,
Or simply to be there
As long as it's night."

And as the time passed
The owl didn't go,
He sat by her side
Until there was snow.

And the world filled with colour
And was no longer grey,
She felt herself change
And night turned to day.

Her heart filled with love
Knowing someone did care,
Though she didn't look up
She knew Owen was there.

And that's when she noticed
Feathers starting to sprout,
All this time she'd been hiding
It was time to come out.

So she pulled back her wings
And saw friendly eyes,
And then her reflection
Oh what a surprise!

She couldn't believe it,
It gave her a fright.
She looked like Matilda
But now she was bright.

And the owl had helped
Re-light the spark,
And saw her shine
When she felt only dark.

And her heart was changed forever
By the kindness of another
Who brought her back from sadness
And helped her to recover.

She glimmered and shimmered,
Such a figure to behold,
She was no longer silver,
Now Matilda, she was gold.